YOU ARE UNIQUE
AN INTRODUCTION TO GENETICS

Biology for Kids
Children's Biology Books

BABY PROFESSOR

EDUCATION KIDS

Speedy Publishing LLC

40 E. Main St. #1156

Newark, DE 19711

www.speedypublishing.com

Copyright 2016

Family reunions happen everywhere and on certain dates. Families gather and celebrate the joy of being reunited as one with other relatives.

We trace our roots and share memories using letters, newspaper articles, pictures, and videos.

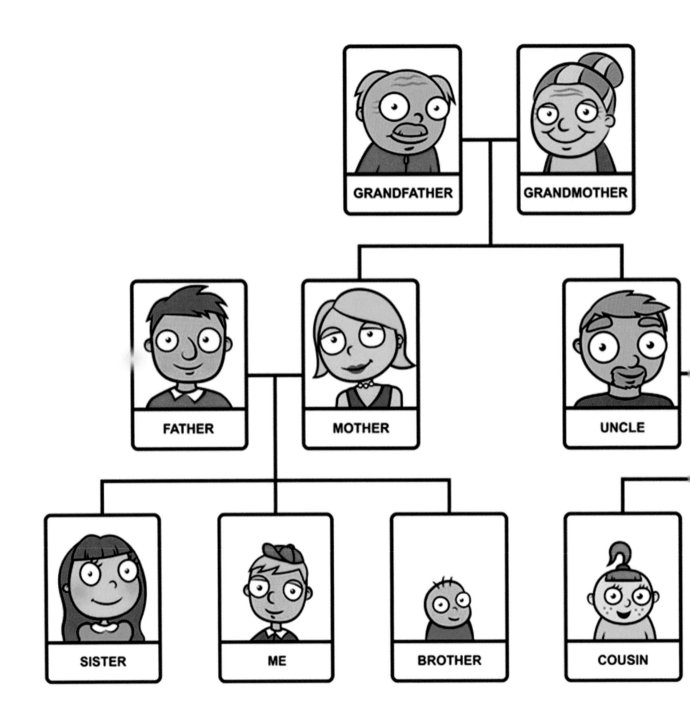

AUNT

COUSIN

Most elders will come up and say, "Look, how tall you've grown!"

"You got your striking bright blue eyes from your dad."

"You're so talented with a knack at dancing."

"It runs in the family."

"It's in the blood/genes."

GENES

Genes are vital and the determiners of our physical traits, like how we look.

You are you and
unique because of the
composition of your
genes.

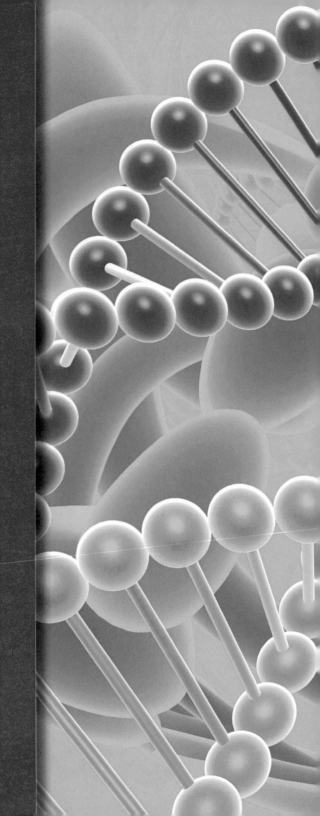

Genes are passed on from one generation to the next in a family, so they also give you your family resemblance. They're like carriers that make you who you are and how and what you look like.

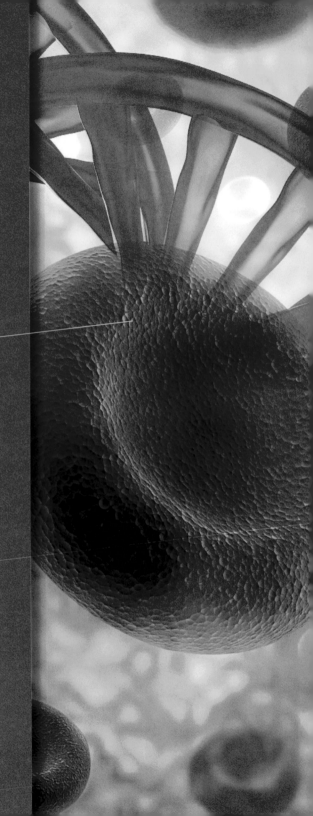

The human body is made up of billions of cells. Each cell contains about 25,000 to 35,000 genes.

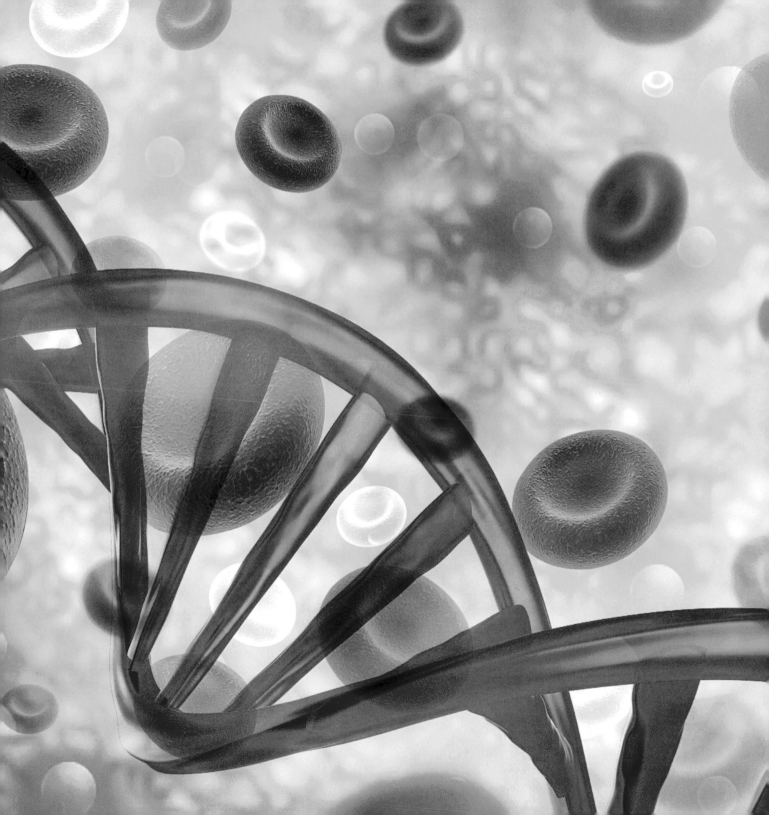

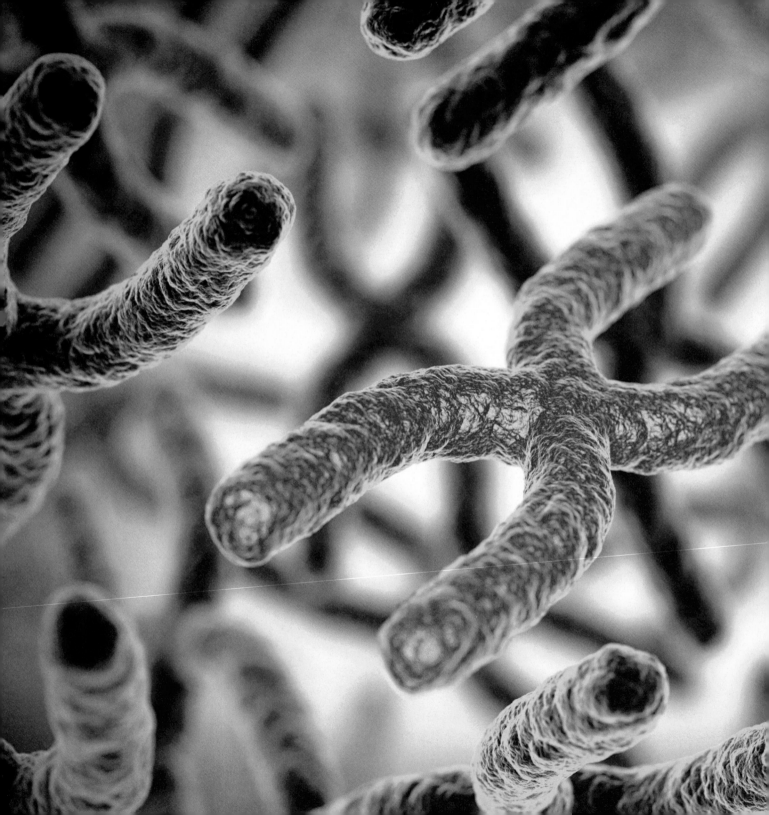

The information carried by these genes determines your traits, features, and characteristics.

Everything is passed on or inherited from your parents, grandparents, or great grandparents.

Genes are also found in all living creatures, both animals and plants.

GENES ARE MICROSCOPIC

These cannot be seen by mere physical eyes. These tiny spaghetti-like structures are called chromosomes. These are found inside the cells.

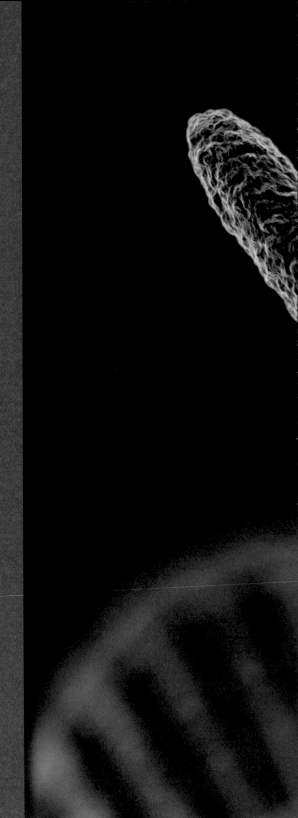

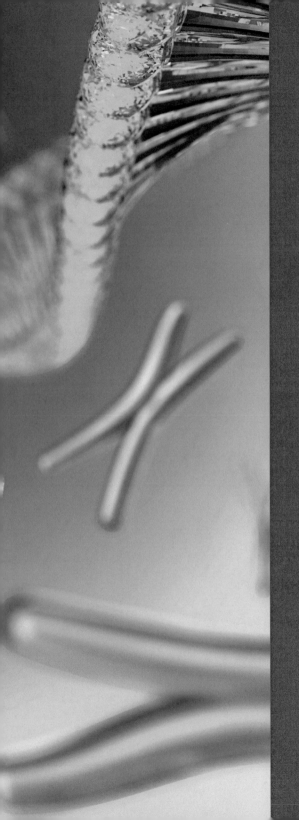

CHROMOSOMES

Chromosomes are in matching pairs. Hundreds and sometimes thousands of genes are in just one chromosome.

The chromosomes and genes are made of DNA (deoxyribonucleic acid). We normally hear or come across this term in sci-fi movies and books.

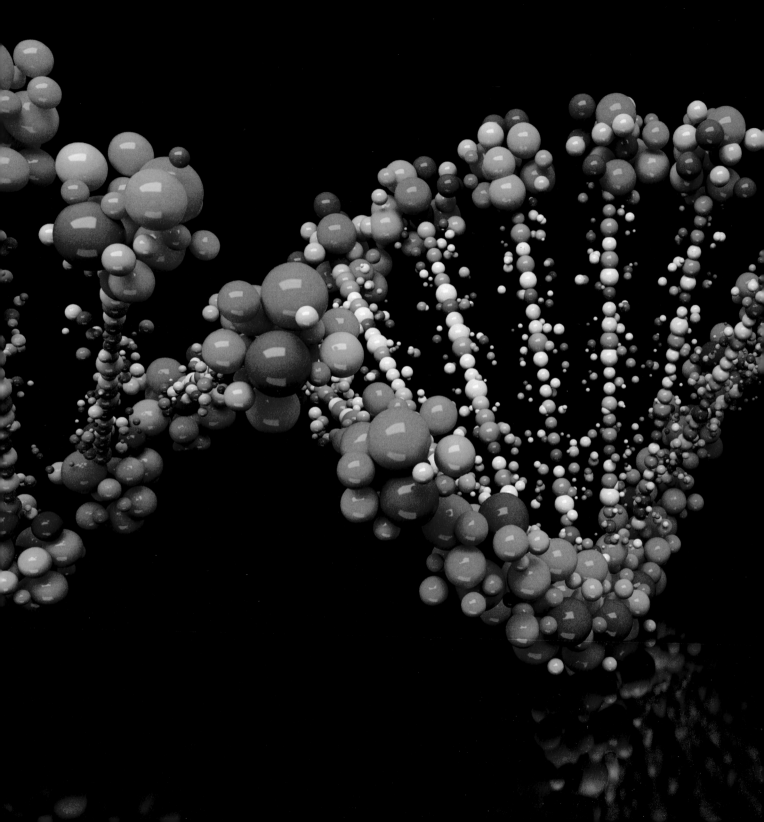

DNA

DNA is a long molecule that contains our unique genetic code. It contains four basic building blocks or bases:

⊃ Adenin (A)

⊃ Cytosine (C)

⊃ Guanine (G)

⊃ Thymine (T)

BASES ARE NECLEOTIDES

These are held together by a backbone that's made of phosphate and deoxyribose.

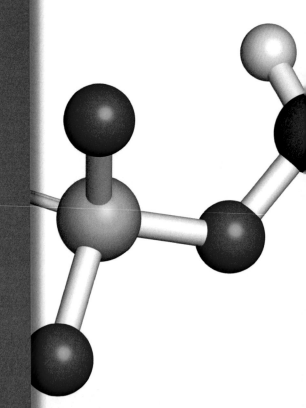

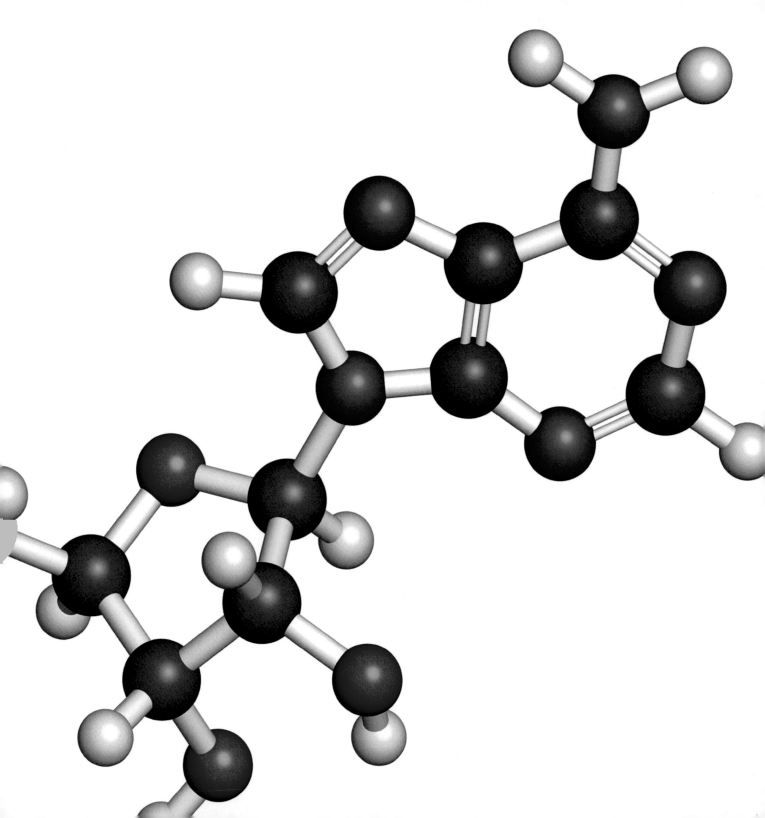

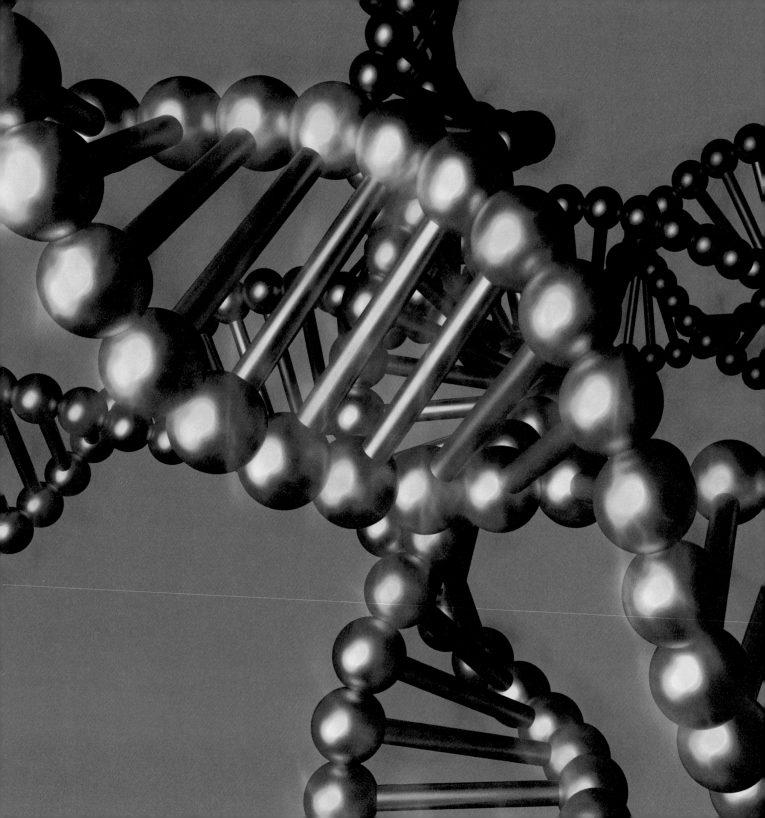

The DNA molecules
may be thousands of
letters long. These four
different letters come
in endless different
combinations.

However, only certain sets of nucleotides can fit together. Like puzzle pieces, A only connects with T, and G only connects with C.

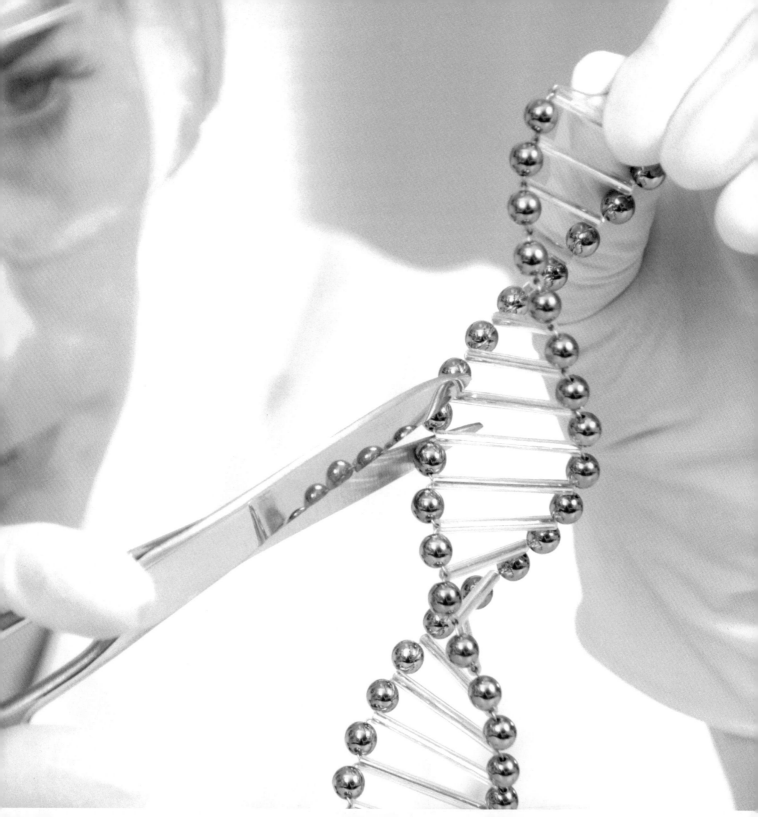

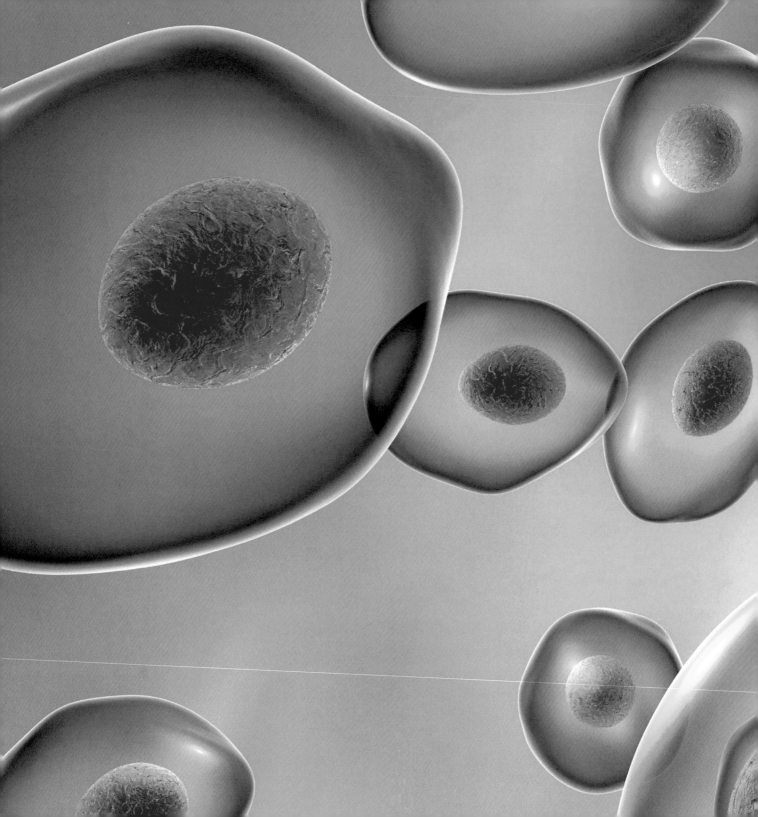

The cell "reads"
the instructions
on the DNA code
that the different
letters represent.
Instructions are given
on how to make a
specific protein.

Proteins are then used by the cells to perform certain functions, to grow, and to survive.

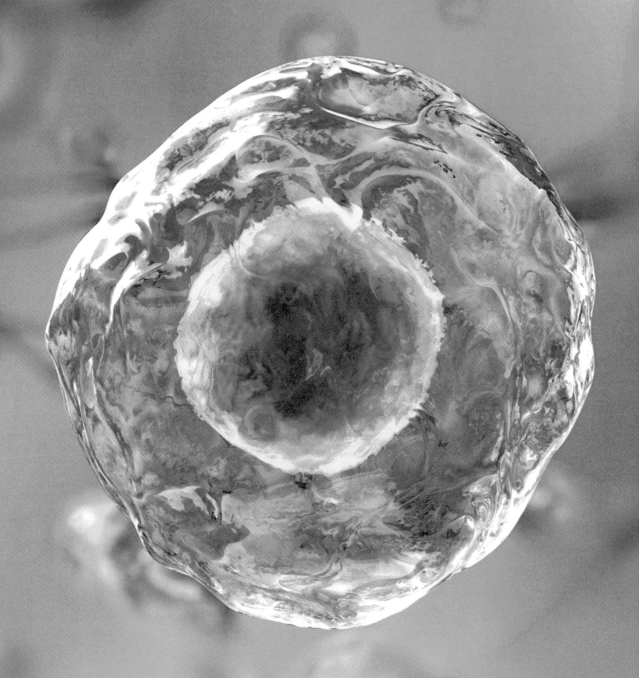

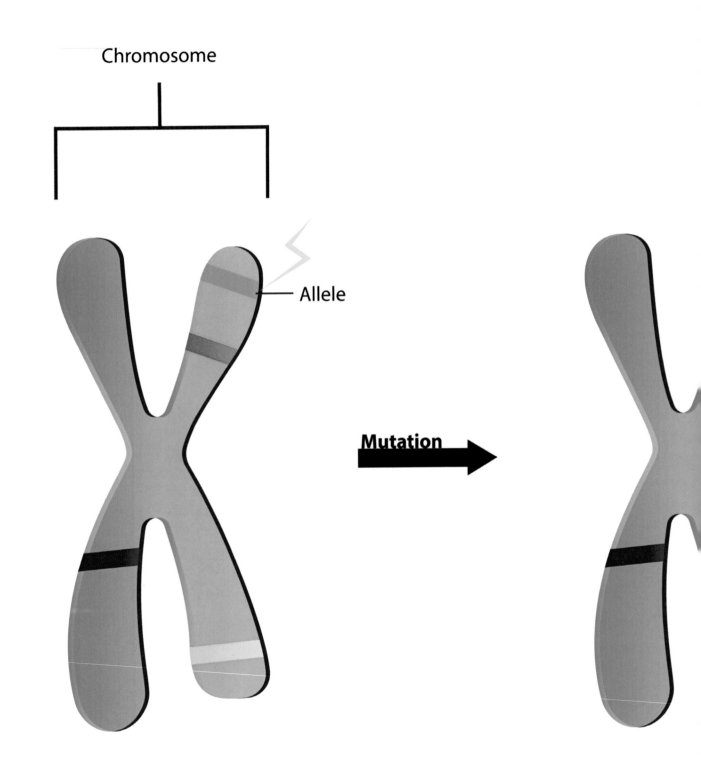

Mutated
allele

ALLELE

While a section of DNA is called a gene, a specific pattern in a gene is called an allele.

For example, a gene determines the hair color. The specific pattern of the hair color gene that causes the hair to be black or blond or auburn (or whatever natural color at birth) would be the allele.

About 99.9% of the DNA of every person on Earth is exactly the same. The 0.1% is what makes us all different from each other.

The genes in the DNA are responsible for passing on certain traits from parents to children.

Some samples of these traits are characteristics such as eye color, height, and athletic ability.

In biology, the study of heredity is called genetics. The basics of inheritance have been discovered by scientists. Genes are actually inherited in certain patterns.

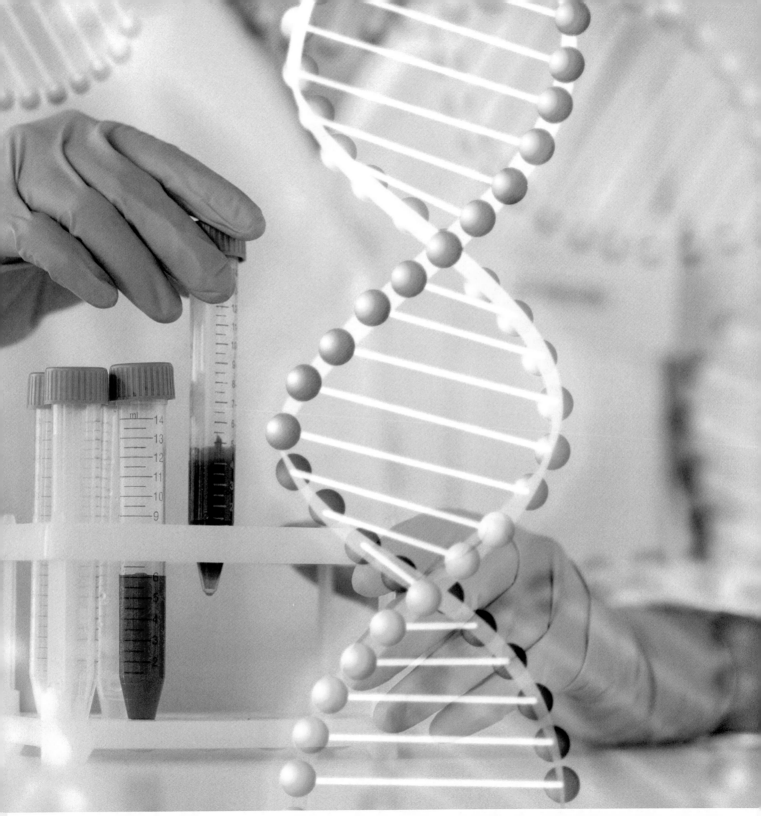

The genes your parents and grandparents have affect what genes you have.

You are unique in some ways but also have something in common with members of your family.

There are two types of genes: the dominant and recessive. Every individual inherits two genes for each trait from their parents. Some are more dominant than others.

Truly, you and I and each person on Earth is unique. This makes human anatomy a fascinating study.

If we were all exactly the same, life would be rather be dismal, less interesting, and even boring.

Made in the USA
Lexington, KY
29 November 2017